MERRICK

JAMES LAMONTAGNE

Published by Unsolicited Press

www.unsolicitedpress.com

Copyright © 2018 James LaMontagne

All Rights Reserved.

Unsolicited Press Books are distributed to the trade by Ingram.

ISBN-13: 978-1-947021-25-9

Cover Design: In-house UP team

Attention schools and businesses. Discount copies are available for bulk orders. Please contact our team at info@unsolicitedpress.com.

DEDICATED TO MY WIFE KARIN.

YOU TEACH ME COMPASSION EVERY DAY

CONTENTS

MERRICK

Proteus Syndrome

When I was thirteen, I rolled cigars
with my one good arm until it gave out.
I was taunted so much
that I used to sleep in the street hungry.

The beatings from father made the perfect misery,
but my head bloomed in a secret place,
an asteroid of lamentations
unpeopled and spared from the hammering.

Mother's eyes were black with beauty
and white with tusks.
I dreamed she was struck down by grayness and trunks.
Her screams became my screams.

I was born in a cloud of low groaned messages
she kept inside. It was her name and my brothers'
and sister's names I whispered at night.
John, (Smallpox) William, (Scarlet Fever)
Marion, (Myelitis).

A trinity of owl pellets cast down into the Oakum.
A white cane cast down on me,

but I huffed my way up the long stairs to the clock,
heaving each second into the smoke:
an incurable exception.

THE HAWKER

On the streets of Leicester he knocked
on the doors that never opened.

Hunger hobbled the cloak
and the broken hip door to door.

From his sack he begged to sell
a country of things no one wanted.

His father beat him for lack of profit.
His would-be customers followed him

with curses and spit balls.
Their faces just as ruinous as his.

The hawker became the hunted
for all their grinding losses.

I followed at a distance
in the shadow of the mercy I forgot to live.

YOU NEVER COUNTED STARS VERY WELL

but you passed all the courses of night:
how much pain the hook of an arm can deliver,
how you survived the death of your family,
connecting all the constellations of sores and stories
into a meal for everyone,
leaving before it caught up with you.
Waking up, a cut
the morning sky sewed together.

HUMBERSTONEGATE FAIR 1862

The fair arrived from Paradise.
We never forgot the roundabouts
though they terrified us.

The wild lions smelled
like earthbound monsters.

At the bazaars there were long rows of tents
with dancers in tights disporting themselves.

Our father avoided them
but the marionettes we did see.

Giants, descendants from the Anakims of old,
a two-ton pig, and India-rubber men.

What matters is how you see them,
soaring or the bogey-man.

During heavy showers
the midgets filled their mouths with gray rain.

5 AUGUST 1869

In the morning the ocean hymned like fire. Walking through the
pitch pines with my father behind the cottage, I whiffed the salt.
He was calm when he was away from the city. I knew something
existed beyond my small definitions, somewhere over the rise of
the cranberry hill, something huge, irrational, with power. Then I
heard it, thunder-like moving through me. My father ran toward
the sound. I looked up, the sea rose above the hill. I thought it
was moving clouds. I knew this wasn't mine. I crouched down
among the hedges' small voices. He ran back to me, What are you
doing hiding like that? Listening to the convocations of being
drawn and being pushed away.

GOING HOME

To Leicester's blackness
and the stink that preceded me
with the young boys who peed on me,
I went back
to the room full of death:
John, William and Marion.
My bed, a make-shift rack
where I held my knees tight against me
as the storm raged in the next room.

I waited for my father to shout
when he learned I didn't bring home any money.
He was light skinned and muscled
from years in the cotton factories,
his hair, black and dirty from the smoky streets.
When he swung down his hand,
I thought at least he cared
something for me.

When he was done
I heard my mother limping after me.

When I was bent over the bridge
she brushed back whatever hair I had
and said I need to be strong.
She led me back to dignity
while I was doing the freak shows for money.

After the drink
he would soften to guilt
and tell me to try harder tomorrow.

PUSHING THE IRON PLOW

Even though I dream
of a raft drifting down the River Soar
you hobble to the haberdashery.

Even though bells rule my life
at the Workhouse,
I wake to the grasslands
you were to me, mother.

Even though you pushed
the iron plow of our lives,
after William died of scarlet fever
all you could do was scratch a cross
on his death notice.

Even though you gave up, mother
and left me at ten,
I created you again
with all that wasn't me
and all you could have been.

Even though father flung
a black tarp over his heart
when he came home from the corset factory.

Even though I was born perfect
you must have thought
you destroyed everything you loved
as I became more twisted every year.

I dream of a tree growing in a canyon
and the scent in the blossom barely there.

WHEN WE BEAT HIM

with the chair legs
we found in the alley
and thought surely he would die,
but he went numb.
He laid there like a stone
as if there were no exits from his body.
We touched the lumps he had
and some we gave him.
We could tell he just wanted to be touched.
After we walked away
he got up and lumbered off
like an elephant hearing
the low sound of his name.

19 March 1880

First night at the Leicester Union Workhouse, dad had to split us
up because he couldn't care for all of us. There were ten in this
little white room. This is the place grandfather Barnabas died 23
years ago. The walls needed a white washing, the gruel was still
there from Esau's bowl. After a raucous night of screams and
beatings, many were sick. In my head the monsters try to push
their way out, but only leave tumors. My dreams are not that way:
I lay down in the cool field of Fasley Hall, where the fox lifts his
red paw. I have to get out of here.

PENNY GAFF

How else can he live?
You don't reason with machines,

pounding down the world.
A hurdy-gurdy plays its ostinato

of monkey music across the smelly street,
across the East Midlands.

Here you could find the clowning.
Here you could find the dancing.

The rotunda on Blackfriars Road was the largest.
We all gave our pennies,

while two women scratched
bloody rivers on their faces,

while we watched the mangled Shakespeare.
Behold, the grace of the forsaken,

but it won't form the rivers needed for us.
The good news of our asking is cheapjack and monger.

'Tis true my form is something odd
but blaming me is blaming God."

DR. TREVES REMEMBERS

I remember the rain falling
on the Dorset Hills --
my first lesson in love.

I remember hiding from Thomas Hardy's sister
behind the coats in the closet at school.

But after graduating
from the Society of Apothecaries
I had a taste for monsters:

Like the two old women fighting
over their dead husbands' clothes.
A man ridden over in the road
with red bone ends sticking
through his trousers.

I first saw "John"
across the street from the London Hospital.
The shop empty and gray with dust,
he crouched on a stool under a brown blanket.

He warmed himself
beside a brick heated with a Bunsen burner.

I, his deus ex machine, carried
him in my Hansom Cab to the bell tower
to sleep, to dream.

I charted every landscape of him:
36 inch round asteroid head
12 inch orbit of a wrist
5 inch round finger.

My operating coat stiff with blood
often followed me home questioning,
am I a good man
or a monster?

PILLAR-BOX HAT

When you pull over
this wild stitching of despair
light still slips through the slit.

You stare out at the churling world
wearing a voluminous black cape
wrapped about you like a Venetian Bravo.

Yes, Treves gave you your own landscape
cradled by the River Soar.
You gulp the air
and the slit of light
brightens your eyes
like small dawns.

MERRICK MEETS GOD

After the examiners leave,
after the investigators go home,
I trust imagination
for what is not seen
like salt licks.

The foxes wander the pasture
searching for what spilled
from the night sky
where nothing is deferred
and the difficult is found.

I wanted you to come down
like a hammer as they did to me,
but instead, Dr. Treves carried
a soft bridle called Meek
through Bedstead Square.

The storms inside beat their wings
and rain me back to longing.
We leave for Fasley Hall.

Frescoes of nails hold the cottage together
but I kiss the walls goodbye.

MERRICK CATCHES A GLIMPSE OF HIMSELF

In the late summer afternoon
the horses drink from the shadows,
sweaty muscled necks
satin black shoulders,
they saunter through the August hay field.
I take a deep breath
and it's all familiar.

An old dream visits me,
a field in shafts of split light.
I come out of the woods weaponless
cured of my griefs
as they run through the high grass.
A new field opened
with a big sky out of the heat.

The sunrays fall harmlessly on me
and on the unimagined beast of myself.
I take another sip of sun.

MERRICK'S SHIP COMES IN

It was time to go
east or north or south
to push against the rains
to migrate my own way.

The traveling life earned lots of money
from all the unbuttoned shows in Belgium.
I look down on everyone
because I'm richer than all of them.
It is all performance and purse
to behold my buffaloed head.

I put my pendulous skin in the game
for a cage with my name on it.

I am the reason many cannot sleep at night
pretending to forget the view.

It grows in the bones, this bitterness.
It covers you at night like a cape.

When they stole all my money
the wind shook the ribs of my cage
and I awoke again to this fierce world.

THE BOXING MIDGETS BEFRIEND MERRICK

They were billed as Roper's Midgets
standing guard over Joe many nights.

Harry rescued him once by knocking out
one of the gang members.
We make our own way, he says.

Joe remembers his own vulnerability,
the seam in his cape,
the hole in the outhouse where he sleeps,
the stress fractures in his neck.

Everyone stares and sees what is weakest,
but the little people talk of spiritual threads,
their soft hungers of all the nights together
and the lost paths of trespasses.

DR. TREVES WELCOMES MERRICK BACK

You've come back to me
my friend, back from Holland
back from being chased
into the recesses of Victoria Station
to live deep within me again.
I struck all the stone streets of White Chapel
and beyond for your name, "John"
but no one answered.
Your eyes are the only truth I see
among your pursuers.
You've come back to me
beaten but still moving.
The police handed me my card
that you kept close to you,
unable to speak.
The woolen factory smoke stacks stopped
burning today.

LEICA MATURIN'S REMEMBRANCE

Dr. Treves said the room at the London Hospital was a prison to
Joseph instead of a home. They wanted to send him to a
lighthouse or an asylum for the blind. So he asked me to visit the
Elephant Man to dispel the darkness around him. Treves said it
was beauty meeting the beast. I didn't agree. When I met him it
was hard not to turn away. He was alone in the basement room.
He graciously shook my hand but slowly released it and bowed his
great head and rested it on his knees and wept.

Dear Miss Maturin,

Many thanks indeed for my grouse and book you so kindly sent me. The grouse are splendid. They keep the loneliness away. The book brings imagination. I imagine your grief to be great with only two months of marriage. I know grief too, but it cannot compare to the loss in your heart.

I must apologize for my behavior when we met in the basement room the other day. It was all too much for me. You were so gracious to me and my heart could not contain it. Please forgive me.

I saw Dr. Treves, on Sunday, whose visits I greatly prize. He is both a doctor and a friend to me. He said I was to give his best respects to you.

With much gratitude,

Joseph

Census Records

This is where pain lives.
Lee Street   Upper Brunswick   Russell Street.
It runs toward him
like school letting out.

He shuts his one good eye
against the pall of misery.

He is as hopeless as a lunatic
with a crowbar prying love from a stump.

This is where pain lives.
Wanslip Street   Churchgate   Sparkenhoe Street.
Above the haberdashery she pounds
on the walls and his broken hip
leaving a mark no one can see.

With no place else to go he lives
at the mercy of the Parish
that has no mercy.

This is where pain lives.
Beck Street   St Anne's Well Road   Whitechapel
She draws pain-maps
on his monstrous head
bosses of bone
the left ear folded downward upon itself
and cauliflower masses of skin.

His hard palate pushes forward and down,
his nose and mouth twisted to the left
because they have no other place to go.

Misshapen fingers crowd
each other to dislocation.
There is no place else to go.

Sleeping On His Back

He was a chronic case.
His voice understood
only by the Thames.

His face covered by his burlap secret.
He knew if it wasn't the practice of perfect misery,
it was music that made things flow.

If it wasn't life giving its daily kick,
it was the theater,
where defenses are built.

If it wasn't a cathedral,
it was a cardboard model of its hypocrisy.

If it wasn't the jagged edge of beauty,
it was his head lifted toward praise
that no one could understand.

If it wasn't his nightly walks by the river,
it was knowing the river passed its burden

on as it flowed by White Chapel.

If it wasn't the awakening in the field,
it was the sleeping on his back that set him free.

His Bones

Michael Jackson tried to buy them
for his private chamber of horrors.
Johnny Depp created a life-size replica of them.
Bowie tried to put meat back on them,
as well as Bradley Cooper.
Leicester called for their burial.
Computers couldn't figure out the algorithm
of his walk.

Your hip joint grieved the left leg dragging it
like a surrogate cane.
The doctors said you were tortured from the inside.
You could weep but you couldn't smile.
Your head was huge
because it was full of dreams.
Your C1 and C2 held up the world,
but snapped when you fell back in your sleep.

The Jack The Ripper doctor
boiled and beached all the bones.
Now you are a mannequin of distortion.

The rest of you dumped
in an unmarked grave in London's east end.

You said once,
in heaven the crooked will be made straight,
and if I were Romeo, we would have gotten away.

Promise Him

His blood shines
among the beatings and the bosses of bones.

Promise him the ocean.
Pour him tea from bone china.

He breathes the world's sorrow.
His spirit is secret and fire.

When he arrives in Hawker's clothes
the gates will burn down.

Remember how we lead ourselves
so quickly to betrayal

of those who walk
the margins of the night.

Some fold his weeping
in their wallets.

Some walk with glass eyes
through a total eclipse.

Some bring him back from the edge
When the body no longer holds up.

What He Wanted Most

I paid the ticket taker of the Penny Gaff
ten times over to be in this show.

What I wanted most was to sleep
like everyone else.

What I wanted most was nothing
broken against my breathing
and the clear boned angel

to lean down to my losses
like lamp light.

Where there'd been a field of flight
there was the wing of a crow.

Where there'd been a dream
there was a black boot in the face.

Where there'd been a family
my pain and clothes were thrown into the street.

Where there'd been a home
there was the fence wire singing to let me go.

Although I am the drifting target of winter
I listen to the blindness of the cold.

The rope broke. The rooms emptied.
I fold my hands to help the angels lift me.

My eyes roll into themselves
with the weight of rivers.

NOTES

This work is a series of poems that Joseph Carey Merrick (The Elephant Man), as well as others, inhabit. The poems generally follow a chronological progression of his life.

The sources used were: *The True Story of The Elephant Man*, by Michael Howell and Peter Ford; *The Elephant Man*, by Sir Frederick Treves; *The Elephant Man*, a play by Bernard Pomerance; *The Elephant Man*, the movie directed by David Lynch.

Proteus Syndrome—Originally, it was thought this was Merrick's disorder, but in 1986 it was conjectured he had this rare congenital disorder also known as Wiedemann syndrome (named after the German pediatrician Hans-Rudolf Wiedemann). DNA tests on his hair and bones in 2003 were inconclusive. He no doubt had multiple problems that contributed to his condition, Proteus Syndrome being one of them.

19 March 1880 —Workhouses were horrible institutions, the last resort for a poor person with no money in the 1800s.

Penny Gaff—A popular entertainment place for the poor of that time. The last two lines are from a hymn by Isaac Watts which Joseph was fond of quoting.

Dr. Treves Remembers—The details of this poem are all factual, but for some reason he refused to call Joseph by his name; he used John instead. He even crossed out his name and wrote "John" on his manuscript about the Elephant Man.

Pillar-Box Hat—His hat still exists at the London Hospital.

Merricks Meets God—Fasley Hall was a private estate near Northampton where Joseph could have the run of the property without restriction.

Merrick's Ship Comes In—Unlike the movie The Elephant Man Joseph was not kidnapped but he "sold" himself back into the traveling circus shows to make money. He was robbed and abandoned in Brussels in 1886.

Leica Maturin's Remembrance—This is a true story and so was the letter Merrick wrote back to her, "Dear Miss Maturin."

Census Records—What is listed here are all the towns and streets where Joseph lived.

About the Author

James LaMontagne studied creative writing at the University of Massachusetts. He worked in Montana as a logger and worked as a church-planter in Massachusetts. He currently lives in South Hadley, MA and works as a Talent Acquisitions Consultant. He loves jazz and has been playing bass for over 30 years. He and his wife, Karin, have 4 children. His poems have been published in many small press magazines. He can be contacted on Facebook and Instagram.

MORE BOOK FROM UNSOLICITED PRESS

Unsolicited Press is a Pacific Northwestern publishing house based in California, Oregon, and Montana. The team started in 2012 and has published more than 70 titles. If you enjoyed reading *Merrick*, then you may want to read:

- ❖ Anne Leigh Parrish's *the amendment*
- ❖ Francis Daulerio's *If & When We Wake*
- ❖ Timothy O'Leary's *Dick Cheney Shot Me in the Face*
- ❖ Adela Najarro's *Twice Told Over*

www.ingramcontent.com/pod-product-compliance
Lightning Source LLC
Chambersburg PA
CBHW070043110426
42741CB00036B/3237